Fierce Protectors
and
Kindly Guides

John Knox McIlwain

Order this book online at www.trafford.com
or email orders@trafford.com

Most Trafford titles are also available at major online book retailers.

© Copyright 2016 John Knox McIlwain.

All rights reserved. No part of this publication may be reproduced, stored in a retrieval system, or transmitted, in any form or by any means, electronic, mechanical, photocopying, recording, or otherwise, without the written prior permission of the author.

Print information available on the last page.

ISBN: 978-1-4907-7635-4 (sc)
ISBN: 978-1-4907-7637-8 (hc)
ISBN: 978-1-4907-7636-1 (e)

Library of Congress Control Number: 2016913588

Because of the dynamic nature of the Internet, any web addresses or links contained in t his book may have changed since publication and may no longer be valid. The views expressed in this work are solely those of the author and do not necessarily reflect the views of the publisher, and the publisher hereby disclaims any responsibility for them.

Any people depicted in stock imagery provided by Thinkstock are models,
and such images are being used for illustrative purposes only.
Certain stock imagery © Thinkstock.

Trafford rev. 08/23/2016

 www.trafford.com

North America & international
toll-free: 1 888 232 4444 (USA & Canada)
fax: 812 355 4082

FOR WENDE AND NOLEN

AND MOTHER EARTH

These poems were written from 2014 through 2016, mostly on the coast of Maine and in Brooklyn. They have been written in collaboration with the spirit guides that have held, protected, and guided me all my life, to whom I bow in gratitude.

May these poems benefit all who read them, and bring them peace and ease of heart. May any merit they may have be dedicated to the liberation of all beings everywhere.

CONTENTS

THE SACRED MOUNTAIN 1
THE WORK OF THE DAY 3
SPIRITS OF THE NORTH 5
THE WHITE SNAKE 7
SUNDAY ZEN 9
THE ANCIENT APPLE TREE 11
THE F TRAIN 13
THE SECRET 15
OUR FIRST MORNING IN MAINE 17
LIFE'S ILLUSIONS 21
STEPPING AWAY 23
THE VISA 27
50 YEARS IS A GOOD START! 29
STONE BUDDHA SAYS 31
WANDERING IN THE WILDERNESS 33
DINNER WITH THE NEIGHBORS 35
NIGHT OF THE FLOWER MOON 37
A SPRING BLESSING 39
A BROOKLYN APRIL 41
HAIKU 43
MONDAY MORNING 45
PRAYER FLAGS 47
GOING FOR A ROW 49
NIGHT OF THE ROSE MOON 53
LUNCH 55
AUGUST 57
THE DOORMAN 59

DANCING WITH THE TREES	63
MORNING	65
DANCING WITH THE FOG	67
TURNINGS	71
A COLD WEST WIND	73
ABOUT TIME	75
MY NEW MORNING WITH YOU	77
GIFTS	79
REST IN LIFE	83
HARBORS	85
TIME FOR A DRINK	89
WALKING BEHIND A POEM	91

THE SACRED MOUNTAIN

Across the wide valley,
Past the snaking river,
Broad shouldered,
Sits the sacred mountain.

In the evening it filled me.
In the morning it brought tears.
"Serve the Great Spirit," it said,
"And I will fill you,
Hold you.
Take the message of love.
Share the one consciousness.
Serve all the brothers and sisters.
Be among them
While I sit silent,
Waiting for the people to come home,
To be held
As I hold you."

I bow and say yes.

THE WORK OF THE DAY

Being emerges
Like the sun rising over the morning hills,
Silencing words that,
Like soaring gulls,
Fill the air.
Mists of night disperse
Displaying in its fullness
The crystal clarity of early day.

For a moment
The sun hangs suspended,
Balanced between the shadows and the light,
All possibilities revealed,
Waters shimmering with love,
Hearts open in wonder.

Then the day progresses
On its appointed tasks.
We forget.
Yet the heart remembers
The fullness
That no words can touch.

But what is our true task
As we seek our broken way
But to find again that Being
That rose like break of day,
And live each moment
In the breathing of our hearts,
To see the rising of the sun
And hear the silence of the center.

The job of life?
Remember to remember.

SPIRITS OF THE NORTH

The Spirits of the North
Bring us the cold winds,
The winds that challenge,
The winds that wound,
The winds of our discomfort.

Honor them,
The wild ones.

They bring us wisdom,
Teach skillful ways,
Demand attention,
Sweeping clean the barns of our sad lethargy,
Bending the tall trees of our arrogance,
Stirring seas that trouble hearts,
Seeking the deeper truths,
The shadows,
The demons that lie below,
Restless, perturbed,
Aggrieved.
Let us bow to the North,
Shout "Ho!"

Open arms and hearts
That dark demons may arise,
Bringing new life,
Breaking old rules.

Bow to the North,
And honor the Spirits of Darkness!

THE WHITE SNAKE

In the dream the White Snake came,
Coiling and uncoiling
About my feet,
Powerful and silent,
Until at last she rose
As tall as me with gaping mouth,
Tongue, teeth and fangs,
Turning to devour me.

I awoke in terror,
Whimpering in fear.
What did she seek?
Who did she seek?

Since that night years ago
Nothing has been the same.
A carapace is peeling back,
Slow shedding of dead skin,
Exposing a soft and opening heart,
Revealing wounds that one by one
Are slowly healed.

Life opening to the three worlds
And spirits of the six directions,
To ancestors, plants, and animals,
The ones that wait for us,
Call out for us to listen and to heed
Ancient wisdoms we've forgotten.

They prod and taunt us,
Fierce protectors and kindly guides,
Steering us from safety and the shore
Into dark of night, the unexplored,
That we might be that which we are,
Beings shimmering in the void,
Knowing ourselves at last,
Swallowed whole by the Snake of our devotion,
The Serpent of our creation.

SUNDAY ZEN

Tribeca loft
Sunday afternoon
Zazen

Cobblestone rumble of cars
Occasional horn
Sun slants
Through drawn shades

Legs crossed
Numb

Back straight
Aching

Breathing in
Breathing out
For hours

Mind wandering

Silence
The master attentive

Breathing in
Breathing out

No reason
No goal
No why
No peace

THE ANCIENT APPLE TREE

The old apple tree calls silently,
Whispering in my heart,
As it watches summer unfold
Up on the coast of Maine.

I almost said "our apple tree,"
For though it sits on land that we,
By common agreement and human law,
Are said to own,
It's only in our arrogance that
We claim this land as ours.

The tree was there long before,
Planted by another generation
For its grace, its beauty, and its fruit,
A promise to the future.

It stands today, a hundred summers hence,
Gnarled arms out stretched, caught mid-dance,
Arched over the small house,
Conversing with the spirits of the land,
Offering us kindness and protection.

How is it that we have been received?
For when we stand upon that ground
We're held by all around
With gentle grace and soft murmurings
Of love and kinship.

Perhaps it was this aged tree
Who brought us to its home,
Reached out for us to join
The spirits of the land
To live in peace among them?

Why else would the spirit of this tree
Call us from afar to feed our souls
Even as we look at other trees
That over reach a small Brooklyn deck?

THE F TRAIN

The F train is a subway line from Brooklyn to Manhattan

Each in our own private worlds,
Held inside,
As the car runs the tunnels through the city,
Weaving the spider's web in darkness.
Books, papers, earphones,
Our own private fears,
Praying silently for safety.
No surprises, no adventures today.

Looking warily about
We rattle on,
Resigned, impatient,
Holding tightly
Against the gnawing beast
Inside.

Or maybe they are happy travelers
At peace with life and with themselves
While I, lost in my own projections,
Let them carry for me my fears,
The demons that lurk within.

Shall I ask them?

THE SECRET

The trees insist,
Waving their tops to the sky,
Blown in windswept dance,
Leaves open, yearning, reaching,
Watch us!
Dance to life with us!
Though the sky may be grey
With scudding clouds,
Watch as we pull life from the earth
And toss it to the sun
There behind the clouds
Awaiting us.

Awaiting you as well,
Brother man, sister woman.
We are but your heart
Springing up for you
Even while you forget,
Imagine yourself alone,
Pretend yourself small.
Your secret's safe with us,
Your glory and your ecstasy.
Remember, it's our secret too,
Which we throw wildly away
For all to share.

OUR FIRST MORNING IN MAINE

We arrived last night,
Road weary and happy,
To a small house on the coast
That greets us with a smile as we pull in,
Car laden with all we think we need.

So many seasons now and it's always new.
The same house welcomes us,
Takes us in with warmth,
And yet
We've never before been here.

Around us the early signs of spring,
Fresh leaves again,
Some bold, some insecure;
So many shades of green,
And bright yellows to shock the eye.
The robin builds her nest again
Right by the kitchen door.
Why won't she ever learn?

Meanwhile, the life around us
Whispers softly on the breeze,
"It's spring again and though we're back,
We've never seen this day.

"You, who've come and gone for years,
Do you know at last you're new?
You, who come from city life,
How open are your ears?

"We, who do not wait,
Wait for you to hear our songs
And the music of the dance.

"You've been out of step, you see,
Stepped on others toes,
Not heard the music playing
More darkly now than ever.
It's been your turn for many years
To step in to the circle,
To whirl and spin, your robes splayed out.

"And while you dance you'll find
That all you'll need is in the air.
For when you stand on Mother Earth,
All you need is in your heart.

"We welcome you to this small house
The same as every year.
Once more it's new again,
Yet it's always been the same.
May you as well be new once more
With open heart and ears,
The sum of all your many selves,
Of all that's past and gone.
Know as well there is no past,
It's but a passing thought.
The future, too, is but a myth.
All you are today and will forever be,
Is all that you'll become."

LIFE'S ILLUSIONS

Slowly the fog lifts
As silence settles in.
A gull laughs,
A lone bird sings.

The harbor's still, the water flat.
There's no one else about.
It's all our own for just awhile
As the tide eases out.

Sitting on the wharf,
Sun warmed,
Feeling the flow of energy.
Land and water
Hold their breath.
Life resting now,
Potent,
Effulgent,
Complete.

To think,
Some god created this universe,
Billions of galaxies all filled
With stars and planets all about,
So on a certain Sunday morning
We could sit in silence

Amidst a beauty beyond words,
Sharing it with trees and birds,
All of life in balance.

What a lot to do so
We could have this blessing.
While galaxies abound in space
With each breath we take
We sit awash in grace.

If, as some have said,
All life's illusion,
Well, then, I say that,
As illusions go,
This one's mighty fine.

STEPPING AWAY

Step by step
The tethers of a mundane world
Release.
A lifetime's career
Ends piece by piece;
Leaves falling from a tree
That's sheltered and held me safe.

When at last the guests
Have left the party,
The room now quiet,
It's time to clean the house
And reminisce.
A sadness of leaving,
Yet the silence welcome.

It's a new time,
A time to rest,
To be restless;
A time to explore new pathways,
Look at life anew.
Nothing to do
But trust;
New life emerging,
New spring leaves,
Another round of guests
To welcome and embrace.

There's tenderness and loss
Like losing the familiar store,
The one across the street,
Where once they knew your name.

But it comes,
The end of the career,
(Hard to even write).
So much life gone,
All memories now,
Good ones and hard as well.
Settling in to a new land,
One without paths.
Like cresting a hill to find
Only fog,
No view ahead.

So step slowly,
Softly,
Listen.
There will be guides
All in time.

Allow the healing.
Honor the pain.
Welcome the loss,
The gift of endings.
For more will come
In their own good time.

Practice letting the wheel turn free,
Look around
For life teems everywhere.
Be grateful for this breath.
Be kind and honor the guides.

THE VISA

You ask, perhaps, where might Nirvana be
And how it would feel to live there?

Well, every now and then
Gratitude for life
Overtakes me,
Overcomes me,
Overwhelms me.

Awash in gratitude,
Submerged in bliss,
I'm granted a visa to Nirvana
To rest a moment in its grace.

50 YEARS IS A GOOD START!

For friends on their fiftieth wedding anniversary.

How many years does it take
To come to know
Myself?
You?
That luminous being that is us?

50 years is a good start,
Time to finish up the preliminaries,
Explore the tender parts
Behind the walls we build
In childhood.
Time enough to raise the kids
And make enough mistakes
For guilt and shame to visit us.
Time enough to pay obeisance to the world,
Play the roles assigned.

Now, preliminaries over,
It's time for the greater mysteries.
Who am I truly?
Who are you truly?
Who is this numinous being
That is us truly?

The mysteries of heart,
Mine,
Yours,
Ours,
And that greater mystery,
The mystery of the Great Heart.

Yes, 50 years is a good start.
Preliminaries over,
Now it's time to begin!

STONE BUDDHA SAYS

On our Brooklyn deck a stone stature of the Buddha sits.

Stone Buddha says,
"Feel me inside,
I'm your anger,
I'm your peace,
I'm your wounds,
I'm your love
And your compassion.

"Wherever you are
Feel me inside
And know
I know
Who you are
Even though you don't."

WANDERING IN THE WILDERNESS

When the Buddha sat under the Bodhi tree
Mara came to challenge,
Bringing demons to frighten, virgins to tempt.

But it was a bad day for Mara.
The Buddha reached down,
Touched a gentle earth,
And fear and lust were powerless.

But what is that to us?
Our demons still torment,
Lust and greed still pull.
Where's our Bodhi tree,
And the Mother's healing touch?

What did we hope to find
When we ate the sacred fruit?
Who was the angry god
Who drove us out of Eden?

We've lost our way in a wilderness.
Our paths go round in circles.
We map the way with minds
That fear a simple truth,
The truth of a quiet heart.
That in all our years of wandering
The home we seek is here.

We are the sacred fruit,
We are the angry god.
We never left the home we seek.

The only thing the Buddha taught:
All are Bodhi trees;
The Earth is holding us
While she awaits our touch,
The wilderness is in our minds
While Eden's in our hearts.

DINNER WITH THE NEIGHBORS

"Do you think," she said last Sunday,
"That as we age and memory fades
We're making room for God,
For the mystery and unknowable?"

After dinner we left and walked
Down through the springtime woods,
As in the east a full moon rose
Still caught among the branches.

Night opened out to us,
Sweet smell of woods at night,
While from the pond
The raucous sound of frogs
Celebrating the return of spring
With a nighttime bacchanal.

At home we walked across the lawn,
Smelled the earth, the grass,
Heard small waves that licked the beach,
Gazed upon those stars that dared
Compete against a clear black sky
With the rising of the moon.

On the wharf we smelled
The waters of the gentle harbor,
Spiced with a salty tang
From off the nearby sea.
In the silence of the night
We heard a distant sound
Of breaking seas far off.

We walked that night
In Eden, God's mystery world,
Idling on our way,
Cherishing the gift of life.

We thought the trade most fair,
To empty out our memories,
So full with lives well lived,
For the magic and the mystery
Of each new moment now.

What better way to walk the path
Leading to that open door
But to open up more room inside
For the grace of woods and moon,
Of sea and stars and the gift of every moment,
This life on Mother Earth.

NIGHT OF THE FLOWER MOON

I stepped outside the door last night
Into the full moon world
And lost myself.

I heard waves breaking on the distant shore
And went back a million years.

I saw the moonlight on the waves
And went back a hundred years.

I smelled salt air from off the ocean
And went back before all time.

Inside, we think the house is ours
But step out through the door
And all at once we are no more,
No sense of who we are.

A hundred layers of life unfold,
The walls of self no more,
No me, no you,
No future and no past,
Just ocean air and the smell of shore
Under a flower moon.

Breeze from the east,
Sky clear,
And in my heart I feel
An ancient pulse of life
So strong, so vast, so free,
I turn away to go inside.

For if the night's so free, so full of life,
Then why does it break my heart?

A SPRING BLESSING

The air this morning is so full
It takes the breath away.

Just days ago the ancient apple tree
Awoke and blossomed out, resplendent.
Then gifted us,
Dropping petals of pink and white
As gentle blessings
That floated down
As we passed by.
Her spring ministrations complete,
She stands now with gnarled branches
Unfolding new spring leaves.

Though the time of blossoming is short
Grace abounds, filling the sweet spring air.

A BROOKLYN APRIL

The trees must love us
More than we do ourselves.
Look at how they awaken,
Spring after spring,
Offering flowers and even fruit,
Gifting us small buds
That soon become full leaves,
While we walk on
Mindless of their blessings.
Do we give thanks?
Do we honor them?

Each day we walk the pavements
Looking down, caught up
With daily lives of gain and loss,
While they reach out to us,
Silently, with care.

So I practice:
Always to walk under trees,
Always to look up,
Always to give a prayer of thanks.

And when I do
I find, just for a moment,
We join in quiet communion,
Opening to oneness once again,
Even here,
On hard Brooklyn streets.

HAIKU

The old lilac tree,
Jealous of the apple blossoms,
Came out this morning.

Lovely as a bride,
Holding her white flowers high,
She belies her age.

The ancient apple tree
Looks down on her with welcome,
Celebrating spring.

MONDAY MORNING

Soft, gentle morning breezes
Lift prayer flags
Carrying songs of peace
Down waking Brooklyn streets.
Across the way
An old antenna leans askew,
Now but a rusting rest for birds
As they go about their day.

Birds chirping, rumble of traffic,
Helicopters overhead.
Yet the city feels at rest,
Not yet in full throated cry,
Still gathering itself to leave behind
The weekend interlude.

How ready we are
To forget our friends,
The trees, the birds,
The sea, the air,
The mountains and the rivers,
Who just yesterday
Embraced us in their healing hearts.

No, today is for commerce,
The work of man.
For a moment, though,
Even as I feel the pull,
I swim against the tide,
Blessed by an unexpected peace.

PRAYER FLAGS

Garish, bright colored
Fluttering squares
Sending out their prayers for peace
Onto the Brooklyn breeze.

The older flags are faded,
Demure and modest,
Calm and quiet,
Their work now mostly done.
But the young ones,
Still bold,
Are brave,
Stand up kind of flags.

Not sure Stone Buddha,
Sitting silent under them,
Pays them any heed.
"The deeper prayer," he says,
"Is just to be, no fluttering,
Rock solid, man."

GOING FOR A ROW

Fog's a tease,
Lurking in the Gulf,
Sending soft tendrils
To the harbor,
And out among the islands.

Will it settle in,
Turn the harbor
To a world of grey
While islands fade away?

Or will it pull back,
Resting on cold waters
Out beyond the reefs?

I'll take the chance
In my small boat,
Put out the oars
And row.
But not among the islands,
Where fog could catch me in a greyness
That chills the bravest heart.

I've been caught before;
Felt fear,
First glimmerings of panic,
Until at last I found my breath
And a shoreline to follow home.

No, I'll row along the shore,
Let it try to fool me there!
I'm no bold adventurer today
If ever I was.
Age brings caution,
Life's too short, too wondrous
To trust a mischievous fog.

The spirits of the sea can be kindly,
But fog is of a darker cast.
So I'll stay close,
Listen to the chatter
Of waves and rocks
In ancient conversation.

I'll glide along the shore
With quiet heart,
Mind stilled
By dip and pull of oars,
In and out like breath,
In simple meditation.

Life balanced
In a small boat,
No one going nowhere,
Floating in eternity.

NIGHT OF THE ROSE MOON

Life is a raw undercurrent
Under ideas
Of right and wrong,
Of wants and fears,
Like gravel in the gut,
Like a river flowing
Under the ice of everyday.

On a quiet night,
Wind off the west warm,
Walk out into the moonscape
And feel the undertow pull on you.

The full moon poised over the village,
Shimmer of lights on water,
Ancient smells off the harbor,
Clear sky, evoking.

Who are we
To stand upon this earth,
Head high,
Caught between now and forever?

Below words is only breath,
Pulse, heartache,
Agonizing sweetness,
Pain of that which can't be said,
Where the mind cracks
And the heart is broken wide.

Oh, Beloved, hold us all, hold us close.
Never forget or forgive
We who yearn to return
Once again.

Why did we leave?

Yet the broken heart makes room
For the fullness of the moon,
Of wind and sea and smell,
For all is complete at last
In a heart broken wide.

LUNCH

Two old friends at lunch
Sitting on a back porch,
Looking over a river as
An eagle flys by.
Sandwiches and soup,
Talking of retirement,
A word that smells of death,
Yet so alive with promise.

Sturgeon leaped,
Ancient fish still full of life
Like us
With aging bodies and youthful hearts,
Wondering where we're being led.
Life not yet through with us,
Gifting us this river beauty,
Abundant, effulgent.

With gratitude we talk,
Step-by-step walking
Deeper into ourselves,
Open, submitting,
To the glory and the grief
That shimmers at the edges, waiting.

All so much, yet
Just lunch with an old friend.

AUGUST

Wandering through another day
You'd think I'd live forever.

Fixed a window, jumped the car,
Read a book and did a puzzle.
Wrote a poem.

Looked out the window at the fog,
And thought about my boat.

Didn't help my neighbor,
Didn't do my yoga,
Didn't meditate or exercise,
Nor even take a nap.
Thought about my book,
And didn't write a thing
(Will it write itself?).

What makes a day?
What makes it worthy?
The finishing of the list?
Or breathing in and breathing out
While looking at the fog?

Perhaps it's how we feel
When it finally comes to end,
And our heart is overflowing
With gratitude and grace.

THE DOORMAN

"You're a door opener,"
She said,
"Just a hunch
But it's what I think."

I said little,
Puzzled,
Pleased,
Intrigued.

Later I wondered,
What the fuck *is* a door opener?

A doorman of the soul?
Like some guy in grey on Park Avenue
Opening doors of yellow cabs?
"What's your destination, ma'am?
Off to heaven again?"

A doula of the soul,
Easing the birth of spirit?
Of heart?
Easing the dying of the ego?

Easing someone on the path?

No books, no teachings,
No one path but the pathless path,
The unbroken circle,
Walking along beside awhile,
Paramedic of the soul.

"Take my arm, sir,
Watch that puddle, ma'am,
Lower your head,
Open your heart,
There's no rush,
Take a deep breath.

"Just remember,
Hell's a passing fancy,
So's heaven.
God's in the air,
Pachamama loves us,
Each and every one,
Her naughty children
So bent on our own weary ways."

To those who'd open doors,
The secret's simple, Rumi said,
No need to beat the door,
No need to ever open it.

We're all inside, you see,
Already home.
Who knew!

You see, my dear,
There are no doors,
Just old stage props
Left behind
By the passing players of the mind.
A gentle scrim,
Illusions of our making.

Around us is
The great blue sky and Father sun,
The diamond sparkling seas,
Life teeming on the land
Where all the doors are open.

Nothing, it seem, for a doorman to do
But lean back and have a smoke.

DANCING WITH THE TREES

Summer trees are joyous,
Exuberant in their leaves.
Buoyant in the breeze,
Nurtured in the earth,
They toss their offerings to the sky.
What do they care of our soul searchings?

Yet they offer us a promise,
An invitation to be gay.
"Dance with us today,
Hear the music in the wind.
Dance for yourselves in joy.
Be with us in this moment.
Exhaust yourselves with laughter,
And while you do, remember
To reach out your arms and hold
The sorrowful, the lost,
The dark ones and the dying,
For the world is always turning.
Some day they'll dance for you."

MORNING

The stillness of
A distant crow.
All at rest.
Sun rises,
Dew dries
While trees wait.
No one about.
The silent breathing of the land.

Let in the quiet.
Open,
Let go.
This moment,
There is no other.

Ripples on the water
Reflect a clear blue sky,
The dark green island.
My body quiets,
Tears come,
And in my heart
A sweet sadness,
Or is it joy?
Let it in,
Let it in,
Let it in.

DANCING WITH THE FOG

There's a fog in from the Gulf of Maine.
Can't see the boats.
Can't see the islands.
Gulls appear from nowhere,
Go nowhere,
Like thoughts.

The only color,
Tattered prayer flags
Sending blessings in the mist
To any and to all.

I could use a blessing
Drifting in an inner fog,
Aimless,
No direction home.

Yet there's grace in that,
A grey grace,
Like the soft air,
The gentle flow of tide,
Stillness inside.

The work of the day
Will be done,
But not by me today.
Don't ask by whom
Or even why.
Just not by me.

Then comes my granddaughter,
Vivid on the dock,
Waving a red fly swatter
To blow away the fog.
I'll watch her,
I'll watch the fog.

Watch it dance
And softly swirl
And listen to its song:

"Be gentle.
Let me dance with you.
Feel soft kisses of the spirits,
The stillness of the center.
Remember,
You're held,
Being taken home,
Nothing needs doing that isn't done.

"Be still.
Cry tears.
Feel pain
Feel love.
Feel joy.

"No matter.
Just be sure
To feel life.
Throw up your arms
Into my heart
And dance with me."

TURNINGS

Gulls float high
On a southwest wind.
A monarch flutters by.
Blue sky, chill air,
Late summer on the coast of Maine.

The season begins its turn,
Early premonitions,
First intimations,
The darkness that is to come
Pulls on the heart
Like the outgoing tide.

A COLD WEST WIND

A winter sun's no match
For a cold west wind,
A wind that tosses the harbor boats
Like stallions fighting to be free.

White caps racing down the harbor,
Steel blue waters, white foam spray.
A gull rides high amongst the winds,
A minstrel and messenger of flight.

Inside the house
It's warm and calm;
The only sound a gentle flute
In the still of afternoon.

So many realities,
Universes intertwining,
Inner tenderness and
Outer coldness.

The falling sun slants in
Casting dark shadows
Against the far walls.
A wooden crow,
Black atop a granite egg,
Casts a quizzical eye,

Standing firm,
Watchful.

Around the room
The art and artifacts of home,
Creations and collections of the years,
Returning now the favor,
Reflecting back our inner richness,
Warming us inside,
Reminding us that even
In the midst of darkness
There is light.

Inner warmth is easily forgotten.
In a moment's kindness
Or in a warm embrace
There's an opening of the heart,
The sounding of the holy name.

The sound that turns the wheel of life,
Offering gratitude
To all for all, and everything.

ABOUT TIME

To think,
Sitting here on this so solid stone,
Ancient, crevassed, weathered,
That we are cousins
Born of a common ancestor,
A magic flash long, long ago.

And more –
That stone and I
Real as we may seem,
Solid flesh and hardened rock,
Are but illusions
Made of empty space,
Quivering points of brilliant light.

Well, cousin,
Fellow mist and dream,
What of cousin water?
Do you two ever talk
As you share caresses
On this soft afternoon?

Why should I
Be the one to talk,
Spilling endless words
Upon the gentle air?

Words with all the weight
And meaning
Of the barnacles
And waving seaweed
That dress you
In such elegance.

And by what perversity,
By what myth and law,
Has it been declared
That all about me
Should be mine?

Who among us,
Descendants all of the cosmic storm,
Has right to call dominion?
What heathen god
Divided the firmament,
Took upon himself
The nonsense
That only one of us would rule?

What if we
And all the cousins,
All the many families,
Rose up as one,
Tossed the old fool out,
Proclaimed the truth,
One heritage,
One past, one future,
One family?

Why the hell not?
Isn't it about time?

MY NEW MORNING WITH YOU

Let me sing a song of wonder,
Fill our hearts with love and grace.

May we dance with joyous rhythms,
Feel the stars weave in our hair
Lacing nets of joy while eagles soar
Above the diamond studded seas.

May we touch the threads of Indra's Net
That hold all life together.
May we feel the gentle beating
Of the hearts of hawks and doves,
See the writings in the sky
That were lost so long ago.

Dance me in the arms of love,
Sing the ancient songs to me,
The ones about creation
And life that never ends,
Of circles and reflections,
And the valleys of our dreams.

Come up, my love, and hold me
While I whisper in your ear,
"This is the miracle and moment,
The morning of our lives,

"Given freely by the Spirit
As the sun climbs up the sky
Blessing all creation
With glory in his eyes.

"A day for us together,
A day for song and praise,
A day to hold each other
And reach with arms of love
For all the many Families,
All creations of the Mother,
Holding all the hearts that hold us
In the mountains and the seas.

"We'll sing the songs the Mother taught
Ten thousand years ago,
And sit in awe and gratitude
For all that lies ahead,
For each breath of life we breathe,
Each step upon the earth,
And remember in our darkness
That the world is always turning
To new mornings in the heart."

GIFTS

The call came years ago
While I was fast asleep.
"Your mother's dying,
Come now."
How was it I didn't know?
The distance between us
More than miles.
My heart cold to you,
Fearful and resentful.

You waited for me,
Unconscious,
Breath rattling,
Knowing I would come.

And I did,
Sat with you,
Held your frigid hand.
Told you finally,
"I love you."
Said all there was in me
To say in those last moments
While you lay silent

Yet hearing still, I pray,
As your son blessed you
And was blessed by you in silence.

As I sat you died,
Quietly, letting go at last.
Leaving yet another gift.

The finest gifts you gave me?
The closing of the circle.
As you were there
When life began,
You wished for me
As you went on.

Were you at peace?
Are you now?
Those cuts I can't undo,
Sharp slices in your heart
Made by the knife I held
In fear and weakness.

You who gave me all you had
Got back so very little.
My heart is broken
But so late.
Can I ever be forgiven?
Or must this heart lie open,
Splayed out,
Picked over by unrelenting guilt?

Is this your final gift,
The teaching of the pain it takes
To stay alive to love?

REST IN LIFE

Outside skies are grey
And winter winds are cold.
Out upon our city deck
Stone Buddha sits,
Dusted white with snow.

Inside my heart
Warm breezes wander in a quiet wood
Where trees sigh softly
While grasses whisper
And silent flowers bask
In sunny glens,
All alive,
Attuned,
Accepting,
Even while surrounded
By the mysteries of the dark.

"Rest in life,"
Was the teaching of the other day.
The master's wisdom:
To accept,
Submit,
Surrender.
Is that the teaching of the forest, too?

For though the sky is grey
And the air is brisk and cold,
The day is rich with simple things
And filled with possibilities.

There is a flow to life,
A river running to the sea
Through the forests of the mind,
Where quiet equanimity
Is found in sunlit fields
When we sit down
And know our work is done
Before it's yet begun.

HARBORS

Outside the harbor
Wind-tossed waves were wild,
Steel grey sea and white foam.
Spray surged against the leeward shore,
While a lighthouse stood
Firm on the ancient point.

Then around the point we drove
Back inside the harbor where
The water's flat and all's secure.
There we sat by the fire at last
Looking out at tethered boats
Seeking safety from the storm.

What is a harbor
But a place that offers respite
From dangers of the sea.

Yet even as we sat
Sheltered from the winds
There were demons breaking free
Escaping from below.

If all must come to light to make us free,
Then what harbors can there ever be?
Storms will find their way around the point,
Rolling waves in from the gulf,
Crashing onto wharves and piers,
Scraping clear all sense of peace.

If fear can find us in our harbors,
Rattle demons in our darkest caves,
Where's safety to be had?

Only that of bold Ulysses
As he headed out to sea.
He rowed out beyond the point,
Leaving the harbor in his lee.
He faced the very dangers
That torment us in our dreams.
It took him twenty restless years
To meet his own dark demons.
Only then, his demons faced,
Was he gently guided home
To find at last the peace he sought
In the land he'd left behind.

So too must we
Sail onto a wind swept sea
And, hand and hand with wild spirits,
Ones of light and dark,
Dance under a blue and loving sky,
Chance our lives upon the waves
Until at last, when hope is gone,
And right and wrong long past,
We find the harbor of our heart.

Then with a gentle wind
We sail for home and,
When to the shore made fast,
We know at last
What bold Ulysses found,
That the only harbor we ever need
Is the heart we always had.

TIME FOR A DRINK

There is fear and sadness,
No words of joy to write today,
I say.

Then, sitting in the park I see
Small children running by,
All smiles and screams
Of afternoon delight.
Their mothers watch with care and love
While trees sway gracefully.
I smile even as the beast inside
Gnaws.

Shadows grow long,
The light softens.
What is there to fear?
It's Friday night;
Must be time for a drink.

WALKING BEHIND A POEM

What is it gives a poem life?
For it's in the first few lines,
Where it comes alive – or not.

New born, it sits unsure
And waits to find its way.
When in time it takes a step,
Then another and one more,
It begins to walk a path
It alone can find.

Step by step, through twist and turn,
It catches this then that,
Weaving all together,
Until at last it comes to rest
And settles in, content.

My job, it seems, is but to follow
As it feels its way about,
To put down words in order that
The path it weaves can once again be found,
A path into the heart, or maybe
This time to the spirits.

JOHN KNOX MCILWAIN

But either way, it weaves a web
That catches life off guard,
And for a moment holds it
For us to see what otherwise
Might never come alive.

Printed in the United States
By Bookmasters